For Donna Smith and for Jan,
best teachers ever;
and for Arnout and Alex, who did it all.
—MR

ca

CHAPTER ONE

The first week of school is always like a yo-yo to me. The up part is being with my friends again. And I do like recess, learning new stuff and going to the library. The down part is losing my freedom. No more sleeping in or taking off on my bike to Mark's house or to the pool.

On the first day of school I found out that Mrs. Cupcake is my teacher this year. Her real name is Mrs. Koepke, but we call her Mrs. Cupcake. I heard she's okay, so that part is fine. And Mr. Smart is still our principal. I always thought that was a funny name for a principal, but I guess he can't help it. Mr. Smart is pretty cool, and there were rumors that he was leaving, so I'm glad he didn't.

I also found out that most of my friends are still in my class. We only have one class for each grade in our school. So I have known most of the kids since kindergarten. Except Tegan, who moved here from another country when we were in first grade. And a girl named Yvonne moved away to the east coast this summer. But other than that, Mark and Mary Jane and Alex and Angela and the others are all here.

On day two we were supposed to learn all about Saturn and other planets. But instead of making us open our books, Mrs. Cupcake told us that she had some exciting news. Mark punched me in the back. It's a habit he has, one I try to avoid whenever I can.

"Hey, Josh, maybe she'll talk until recess!" he whispered. I grinned at him.

"I have something very important to tell you!!" Mrs. Cupcake beamed. I noticed that whenever Mrs. Cupcake gets excited, she beams—not unlike my baby sister, Angie, when she's done something on her potty.

"Well," started Mrs. Cupcake, sitting on the edge of Jesse's desk, "as you probably know, it is a custom that this class goes on a special field trip."

Oh yes! This was going to be good. This was what I was waiting to hear. Of course we all knew about the annual field trip!

"Each year," Mrs. Cupcake continued, "our Parent Advisory Council sponsors the trip and our teachers volunteer their time so that the class can go. This year we are heading to Drumheller!"

My mom is on the Parent Advisory Council. Here, finally, was something she did that was worthwhile. Everything else was mostly embarrassing. Like showing up in the gym when we had an all-school assembly, or going to the school board to complain about the fact we didn't have enough instruments for everyone in music class and things like that. But if my mom was getting us to Drumheller, that was all right.

"Is that in Arkansas?" asked Dudley Jones. We mostly call him Dud.

"No, Dudley." Mrs. Cupcake sighed. "Drumheller is in Alberta. It's about a six-hour ride on the school bus."

Holy moly! Six hours on a school bus. I didn't know if I could handle that. Twenty minutes every day was bad enough, especially when the third graders were singing "The Never Ending Song." But the third graders weren't going on this field trip, so we might be okay.

"Now, of course you know that Drumheller is famous for its dinosaur museum. We'll be seeing dinosaur bones, dinosaur replicas, other fossils—all sorts of exciting things!" gushed Mrs. Cupcake. "We will be studying this topic in great detail before we go."

Mark rolled his eyes at me.

"You will have a chance to do research into different kinds of dinosaurs. We will make a dinosaur collage, and you will be writing dinosaur stories!"

She made it sound as if we were lucky that we would get to do schoolwork.

"But—"

I knew there would be a *but* to all this.

"—we need to raise money to be able to go."

Great. There had to be a catch to going on a big field trip. They wouldn't just let us go and have fun for a week. We'd have to work for it and earn it first.

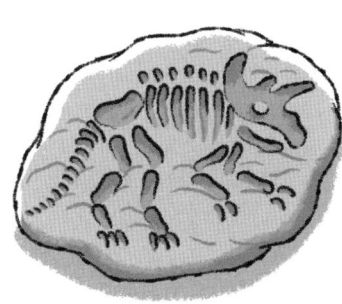

CHAPTER TWO

Over the following months we made papier-mâché dinosaurs, and everything got covered in goo. I forgot there was thick goo on my hand and rubbed my hair. Mark looked like he had scales. Angela's table got covered in guck, and so did the floor. But the end result was awesome. We put a green piece of plywood on the floor and had dinosaurs "grazing" on it—a *T. rex*, a *Spinosaurus*, a *Diplodocus* and a *Brachiosaurus*. There was also a *Stegosaurus* that looked like an elephant with spikes.

We made pterodactyls and hung them from wire coat hangers. Some looked more like bats with giant teeth, but it was cool to see them dangling from the ceiling, especially when the window was open and they moved in the breeze. I even learned how to spell *pterodactyl*!

We ended up talking about dinosaurs all day, every day. Our librarian, Mrs. Pringle, brought us her entire collection of dinosaur books. We studied dinosaur bones in biology. We talked about prehistoric times during history. We measured and counted dinosaur bones and dinosaur teeth in math. The only thing our teacher did not have us do was write dinosaur poems.

Mrs. Cupcake had posters of dinosaurs all over the classroom. One said *Dinosaurs didn't read. That's why they became extinct.* My favorite one showed a bunch of dinosaurs smoking. It said *The real reason why dinosaurs became extinct.*

We watched dinosaur movies and had dinosaur tests. It was almost too much of a good thing.

But even if we learned all we could before going to Drumheller, we still needed to fundraise.

"A trip like this will cost lots of money," said Mrs. Cupcake, looking around the room as if it was our fault. "We have to pay for the school bus and driver that will take us there. We need to buy meals for a week and arrange for a place to stay, and we have to pay entrance fees for the museum and the tours."

"What do we get to eat?" asked Jesse. He's always concerned about eating. I don't think Jesse ever stops chewing. Maybe he's part cow. At recess, at lunch, on the bus, even just sitting in his desk, Jesse is always chomping on something.

"Well, on the way we'll stop in Calgary. We do that every year. Last year we stopped at a very good pizza place." Mrs. Cupcake smiled. "And in Drumheller we can have our meals in the camp we'll be staying at."

Jesse seemed content already. He wouldn't care about dinosaurs. As long as we stopped at the pizza place he'd be happy.

A practical question popped into my head. I raised my hand.

"Yes, Josh?"

"How will we raise the money?" I asked.

"I'm glad you asked." Mrs. Cupcake jumped up from the desk and began pacing back and forth in front of the classroom. "We need to come up with some new ideas. I mean, we simply can't go around selling any more chocolates."

We all chuckled. Someone selling chocolates had come to every house at least twice in the past few weeks. Pleasant Valley is a pretty small town, and we have three schools close together. When one school does a fundraiser, they always hope the other schools won't be doing the same thing. But this year one school chose to sell chocolate-covered almonds and so did a hockey team. The 4-H Club had sold chocolate-covered mints, and the Scouts had just finished selling cream-filled chocolates for their fundraiser! The whole town had been chomping on chocolate-covered almonds and chewing chocolate mints for weeks now. There were boxes of chocolates on the counter in the bank and at the checkouts in the grocery store. There were even baskets full of boxes of chocolate-covered almonds in the hardware store. No, selling chocolate was definitely not an option.

"Also, we don't want to sell gift wrap," Mrs. Cupcake added. "Our school sold gift wrap last year just before Christmas, and our Parent Advisory Council decided that it really wasn't very environmentally friendly."

That sounded like my mom, all right. She was always telling me to get out of the shower fast, because using up all the water wasn't environmentally friendly. You'd think I was doing my environment a favor by taking a shower.

"How about a pizza sale?" asked Jesse. Self-interest.

"Well..." said Mrs. Cupcake. She said *well* a lot. If we got a dime for each time she said *well,* we probably wouldn't need to fundraise for our trip. "Well, I think we should think of something more unique. Something our community needs. Something that can be a community service as well as a fundraiser."

"Selling pizza would be a service to the community," Jesse insisted.

Mary Jane raised her hand. "How about selling things people can use for Christmas?" she asked.

"Now there's a good idea," Mrs. Cupcake said, smiling. "I know the

Parent Advisory Council has catalogs from companies that have things we could sell door-to-door. I'll ask them to drop some off so we can all have a look at them to see what we might choose to sell that people can use for Christmas."

"How about a book sale—a used-book sale?" asked Angela.

"Or a garage sale! I have lots of junk at home I can bring," volunteered Mark.

In the end we sold Christmas ornaments door-to-door. It wasn't that much fun, but people bought them, and we did end up making a lot of money. We also had several car washes, which were lots of fun, and a few cupcake sales. We put a jar of jelly beans on the counter in the school office. If you wanted to guess how many beans were in there, you had to pay a dollar, and if you were right, you could win the whole jar. All the kindergarten kids wanted to win it, so they made lots of guesses. My favorite way to make money was when we had a sale in the gym. I brought lots of old stuff to school, including my old comics and a plastic train track that I outgrew a long time ago. I bought Adam's old comics and Tegan bought mine. I bought some of Angela's DVDs and a karate medal. Mostly we all ended up taking each other's stuff home.

Finally we had raised enough money. The Parent Advisory Council matched our funds, and by the end of the dino-filled school year we were ready to go on our week-long field trip to Drumheller!

CHAPTER THREE

"Why can't I bring my iPod?" Alex whined when Mrs. Cupcake told us we were not allowed to bring electronics on our field trip.

She sighed. "We're going unplugged," she said. "Old-fashioned talking to each other and going on hikes."

Mark and I were excited when we finally started the real preparations for our trip.

"Make sure you pack everything in one small suitcase or backpack. I don't want to see luggage as if you're going to Europe for a month!" said Mr. Jenkins, our math teacher. He would chaperone the boys. Mrs. Cupcake would look after the girls. One mother, who was a nurse, was coming to help. I was glad it wasn't my mom.

Mr. Jenkins gave us a list of what to bring. "And be here Monday morning at 6:00 AM. The bus leaves at 6:15 sharp!" he warned.

We moaned and groaned. I have never even seen the world at that hour. I packed my things on Sunday. Pants, a sweater, underwear, that sort of stuff. I took a flashlight, just in case. And essentials, like comic books. And my baseball cap. Then I went to bed early and set my alarm for 5:00 AM. Yikes.

It seemed like the middle of the night when the alarm went off. I pounded on the clock and turned over. Two minutes later my mom shook me awake.

"If you don't want to miss this field trip, you better get going!" she said.

I tore myself out of bed and stumbled into the shower.

I was still half asleep when we got to school. It looked weird—everybody was there, but it was barely light outside. The school bus was waiting. I was glad to see that Mr. Harmsen was the driver. He's cool. He doesn't constantly yell at us to be quiet.

Mark came running up as soon as we parked. My mom opened the back of the car and I lifted my bag out. "See ya, mom!" I waved. But she came over anyway and had to give me a big hug, and a kiss, right in front of everyone.

Jesse was there, and Adam too. His dog, Picasso, ran around the school grounds. Whenever he came close to the pile of luggage, all the girls started to scream. Picasso had a habit of peeing on things.

As soon as Mrs. Cupcake said it was okay, we boarded the bus. Mark and I sat close to the back. I pulled out some gum and settled in for a long ride. "Man, I don't know about this," Mark sighed. "Six hours on this bus!"

"You'll get used to it," I said, taking the top off my bottle of grape soda.

"Is that your breakfast?" Mary Jane asked, wrinkling her nose.

"Let's count heads!" Mrs. Cupcake called from the front of the bus. "Who isn't here yet?"

Of course, several kids said, "Me!"

I looked around. "Dudley," I said. "Has anyone seen him yet?"

"Dudley isn't here yet, Mrs. Cupcake!" Mark yelled. Just then an ancient Jeep pulled up behind the bus, and Dudley tumbled out. His dad, a tall skinny man with a long ponytail, hauled an old suitcase toward the bus.

"Hey! He's here!" Adam yelled.

As soon as Dudley was on board, Mrs. Cupcake counted heads again. Then Mr. Harmsen started the bus. Pretty soon we were rolling out of the school grounds.

Picasso chased the bus, and parents waved.
We were on our way to the Badlands.

CHAPTER FOUR

By the time we had been driving for an hour, we were all sick and tired of the bus. And Angela really was sick. She was sitting in the front row, looking green, with her nose in a plastic bag.

My grape soda was all gone. Mark's chips were finished, and we were getting pretty bored. Mr. Jenkins was telling riddles near the middle of the bus, but I couldn't hear what he was saying.

"This is gonna be the longest trip of my life," Mark complained.

We played Rock, Paper, Scissors. We talked about cool bands and played cards. We played My Grandmother Is Weird and tried to spot license plates from faraway places. We talked about things we usually never talk about. When we're at school, things seem different. Now we had time to just talk. I didn't know that Jesse's dad was a policeman or that Angela had an aunt who lived in Africa and that Angela had been there. Dudley's dad was really different from most of our fathers. He was a pacifist who went to protest meetings to prevent forests from being cut down and things like that. "We live out of town because my parents want to live off the land," Dudley told us. And I didn't know that Mary Jane's parents were divorced.

When we drove through a town, we read advertisements on signs and looked for stores we knew. Mr. Harmsen had given us strict rules about not leaning out of the windows, but Jesse stuck his head out and yelled at a motorcyclist. Mrs. Cupcake nearly had a heart attack and told him she would send him right home if he did it again!

I think I must have dozed off, because I woke up with a start when the bus went over some bumps in the road. We were getting close to Calgary, on a long straight stretch of highway, the snowcapped Rocky Mountains behind us. Fields on either side had little in them but tumbleweed. Suddenly I heard Mr. Harmsen swear really loudly. I thought I saw sparks flying over the hood of the bus. The bus swerved, waking everybody else up, and Mr. Harmsen pulled over and stopped, tires screeching.

"What's going on?" Mark asked.

"I dunno. Something's wrong with the bus."

The bus was stopped on the shoulder of the highway. Mr. Harmsen yelled, "Everybody out!" We all jumped up and tried to get to the front door at the same time. We tumbled out and stood in the field beside the road. Thick, black smoke billowed out from under the hood of the bus. Mr. Harmsen opened the hood, and more smoke spewed out. He swore again. Mrs. Cupcake looked very upset now—she didn't like the smoke or the swearing. She tried to herd us into one spot on the field as if we were a flock of sheep, away from the highway and out of earshot of Mr. Harmsen. Mr. Jenkins

was peering through the smoke, trying to determine a cause. Mr. Harmsen started kicking the bus's front tire.

"I was afraid this bus was too old! They should have known this could happen! I told them so!" he muttered. Mr. Jenkins tried to calm him down. We sat down among the tumbleweeds. I glanced along the highway. Not a house or a gas station in sight.

"Maybe we can hitchhike the rest of the way?" Jesse suggested hopefully.

Mrs. Cupcake was working hard on restoring her good mood and optimism. "I'm sure we'll be on our way again soon!" she said brightly.

Suddenly a police car appeared over the hill in the road. It pulled up right behind the bus and turned on its flashing lights. This was getting interesting.

We crowded around the officer who unfolded herself from the cruiser. "Trouble?" she called to Mr. Harmsen, looking at the black smoke that still rose from the front of the bus.

"No," Mark whispered to me, "we're having a picnic and roasting wieners under the hood!" I punched him.

Mrs. Cupcake tried to usher us back into the tumbleweed. The police officer had a conversation with Mr. Jenkins and Mr. Harmsen and scratched her head. Then she went to the cruiser and talked on the radio for a while. "Help's on the way, folks. Someone from Calgary is bringing a new hose."

We sat down in the dry grass again. I sure hoped it wasn't poison ivy. We counted cars that came by. First all the red ones, then all the silver ones.

We tried to spot Vipers and Lamborghinis. Suddenly Jesse screamed!

I jumped. He pointed, speechless, at the farmer's field behind us. A huge brown bull was sauntering toward us.

"Oh, how cute!" Mark yelled. "Here, cowie, come here!"

"It's a bull, dumbo," I said. "Bulls aren't cute!" The bull came closer, his head lowered. His beady brown eyes took in the school bus and all of us. He stopped and snorted. Even Mrs. Cupcake yelped. The bull looked at her and scraped his front foot on the ground. Dust flew up. We all huddled closer together and edged back toward the bus. I surveyed the fence between the field and our group. It didn't look like it would be much of an obstacle to the bull. The bull snorted and scraped again, sending up a cloud of dust.

"Ha-ha-ha-tchoo!!!" Dudley sneezed so loudly we all jumped. So did the bull. In fact, he turned around and thundered back over the hill in the direction from which he had come.

"Way to go, Dud!" someone said. We slapped his shoulder. Dudley had never before been complimented on his sneeze and looked quite pleased with himself.

Finally the maintenance person from Calgary arrived, and he worked on the bus with Mr. Harmsen. They hammered and clonked under the hood for a long while. "All done," they finally announced. By now we were all very hot and tired and starving and way behind schedule. We climbed back on the bus and had to keep going without even stopping for pizza. Jesse was super mad.

CHAPTER FIVE

By the time we finally made it to Drumheller, it was really late. At least Mr. Harmsen knew how to get to the campground we were staying at. *Dino-Site*, the sign by the entrance read. We stumbled out of the bus and stood sleepily in the middle of a circle of little wooden cabins. By the light of the moon we could tell that there were no trees around, just dusty ground and some cabins. Mark, Jesse, Dudley, Adam, Alex and I were assigned to one cabin. I got a top bunk. We didn't bother brushing our teeth or anything. Just rolled into our bunks and tried to sleep in the unfamiliar cabin.

As I tried to get used to the lumps in the hard mattress, I listened to the strange night sounds. The darkness hung over the cabin like a blanket. It was much warmer here than at home. It smelled different too. Suddenly I heard a mournful cry in the distance.

Something scraped against the wooden wall of the cabin. I sat up straight, almost bumping my head on the ceiling. One of the other boys turned over. "Did you guys hear that?" Jesse whispered.

"Yeah," I replied.

"That cry. It—it sounded awful. Like a ghost."

"That was no ghost," Mark scoffed. "I think it was a coyote." He didn't sound very sure of himself though.

"I know what that was," Dudley whispered.

"What?"

"A dinosaur!"

We all laughed out loud. "You dodo! There are no real dinosaurs here."

"Why don't you ever hear it when pterodactyls go to the bathroom?"

"I don't know...why?"

"Because the pee is silent!"

Adam snickered. "Go to sleep, Dud!"

We all tossed and turned a bit more. I tried to imagine dinosaurs roaming

around outside. They'd be taking slow, heavy steps, leaving footprints in the dry dirt. And swinging their heads from side to side.

A low snoring rose up from the bunk below me. Everyone else had fallen asleep, but I just lay there, listening to the hollow, distant crying that continued well into the night.

When I woke up it was pouring rain. A steady, gray, warm rain. It turned the campground into a slippery field of mud. After breakfast in the camp cafeteria, we boarded the bus to the Royal Tyrrell Museum. Groups of tourists crowded in front of the museum, taking photos of everything. A museum interpreter met us at the entrance.

"My name is Sandra, and I'll be your guide. Now, I'd like you all to stay together, and if you have any questions, please let me know!" She led us through the museum and into the first exhibit hall. Enormous dinosaur skeletons towered throughout the hall, from the floor to the ceiling, gazing down at us. There were fake palm trees and rock formations. In the distance I heard muffled roars and spotted a display of dense rainforest. There were rumors that there was even a woolly mammoth lurking somewhere in the museum.

Dudley asked about the sounds we'd heard in the night, and Sandra confirmed that there were lots of coyotes around Drumheller.

As we toured, Sandra launched into a detailed description of how dinosaurs lived, what they ate, how and where their bones were found, how skeletons at the museum are being reconstructed and much more. I tried to see how the bones of a skeleton were actually held together, but I couldn't see anything! It was pretty cool. After she talked more about the digestive systems of dinosaurs and theories of extinction, she asked if there were any questions.

Angela put up her hand. "Where's the bathroom?"

We saw every possible kind of dinosaur that ever lived. It was really neat, especially the great big ones. They had enormous jaws. Some had horns. It was strange to think that these huge animals had really roamed this very spot once.

There were dinosaur footprints, even fossilized dinosaur eggs. "I heard of some kids in Australia recently," Dudley said to Sandra, "who found a real dinosaur egg!"

"That's right," Sandra replied. "They found it while digging just outside their town. And the Museum of Natural History paid them good money for it."

"Cool," I said. "I wouldn't mind finding a dinosaur egg!"

"What if you did?" Sandra smiled. "What would you do with it?"

"I'd keep it!" Mary Jane yelled. "I'd keep it and hide it in the basement! I'd keep it warm in a pile of blankets and hatch it!"

We all laughed at the thought of hatching a dinosaur egg and having a baby dinosaur living in your basement.

When we got to the museum store, Sandra said goodbye and told us to enjoy the rest of our field trip.

We left the museum through the gift shop. Mark and I tried to decide what sort of souvenirs to bring home. There were bowls in the shape of dinosaur footprints. Mark wanted one of the balsa-wood model-building kits of a *Tyrannosaurus rex*. I liked the glow-in-the-dark T-shirts, but they were too expensive. I bought some chocolate-covered "dinosaur droppings" for my mom and a postcard to send to my grandma. We unrolled posters to see what they looked like until we discovered that there were sample posters hanging on the wall. I choose one of a *Stegosaurus*.

Dudley bought a back scratcher in the shape of a dinosaur claw.

When we finally came out of the store, Mrs. Cupcake and Mr. Jenkins were counting heads. Mr. Jenkins went back into the store and came out all agitated. "Where's Jesse?" he asked.

I hadn't seen Jesse since the *Brontosaurus* display. Mrs. Cupcake sent

Mark to check out the washrooms. No Jesse. We retraced our steps through the whole museum. No Jesse. Mr. Jenkins went through the store again. No Jesse. This was getting to be a real drag, since we wanted to go to the research fields.

Where would I be if I were Jesse? I wondered. "Let's check the cafeteria!" I suggested. Sure enough, Jesse was sitting in the cafeteria, a tray loaded with chocolate milk, a donut, an order of fries and a piece of apple pie in front of him. He was quite surprised when Mr. Jenkins started to yell at him.

"I didn't need to be in the store," he protested. "I needed to eat."

We all ended up having fries and burgers. And then we finally went outside for a tour of the badlands.

CHAPTER SIX

By the time we left the museum the
rain had stopped. But the sky was still
heavy with gray clouds, and everything
was dripping wet. We got on the bus
and Mr. Harmsen drove us to our
next destination. There we had to get
on another bus because the site was
restricted to the park's own tour busses
only. A guy named Jeff was our driver
and tour guide.

"Since it has been raining so badly," Jeff warned us, "you will have to be very careful where you walk. It doesn't rain often here. Rain turns these trails into slippery mud and can also cause flash floods."

I looked out the bus window. Huge stone mushrooms towered everywhere. "These are the hoodoos," Jeff explained. "They are layers of sandstone that erode at different speeds. The tops are made of a harder kind of stone than the parts underneath that eroded away. That's why they look like mushrooms."

Jeff pulled over near something that looked like a small house. It turned out to be a shelter with a roof, with two walls and glass windows underneath. Inside the shelter you could see dinosaur bones as they were found, still in the ground and partly covered.

"Imagine walking here and finding them," Mark said to me as we stood looking at the bones. The bones were brownish and big.

"I don't know how you'd know they were dinosaur bones," I said. "You'd think they were just cow bones or something."

"Back on the bus, guys," Jeff called. "Soon you'll be able to go for a walk and get some exercise." He had been talking to Mrs. Cupcake, and I think they'd decided we had been cooped up long enough and needed to burn off some of our energy. At the next stop we looked at more dinosaur bones in a display. There was also a large metal dinosaur that little kids liked to climb on and have their picture taken with. Little kids, but us too. Mary Jane and Angela wanted Mark to take a picture of them on the dinosaur.

"Go farther back, Mark!" I yelled. He took a big step backward.

"More," Adam yelled.

"No!" cried Angela, making Mark look behind him. One more step and he would have slid down the embankment. It wasn't very steep, and it would have given us a good laugh to see Mark slide down.

"All right, everyone," Mrs. Cupcake said, "you can go for a hike among the hoodoos here. Follow the path and stay on it. I will expect you all back here in thirty minutes." She looked at her watch.

"It's a round-trip trail," Jeff added. "You can't get lost, but there is a bit of a drop-off on one side as you go around the cliff, so make sure you stay on the trail."

We all took off in small groups. We had been herded around in a large group long enough. Mary Jane, Angela, Mark and I started off together. First we were almost jogging, but we soon slowed down because the trail started to climb steeply. It was still wet from the rain and pretty slippery. Mary Jane was looking at the wildflowers that grew here and there in clusters. Dudley stayed behind, howling for coyotes and looking for things to photograph.

Mark kept stopping to bend down and scrape the dirt. I'm sure he hoped to make an earth-shattering discovery at any moment. "Maybe we'll find a kind of dinosaur that wasn't known until now," he said hopefully. "There ought to be bones here!"

"Yeah, and they'll call it the Markosaurus!" I laughed.

I walked on, trying to catch up to Mary Jane on the curving, narrow trail. Suddenly I heard a blood-curdling scream. I jumped and looked to where Mark and Angela had been behind us just a few moments earlier. There was no one to be seen.

Mary Jane and I ran back down the trail and around the bend. Mark and Angela were on a ledge halfway up the steep cliff face above the trail, clinging to the wall of dirt and rocks. Angela had her hand clamped over her mouth, and Mark was screaming bloody murder.

"What? What happened?" I cried.

They looked at us, relief showing on their faces when they saw us. "Heeelp!"

Angela cried softly, pointing down to the ground near her feet.

"What?" I called.

"A sssnake!" Mark managed to croak. I could make out the faint, dark outline of what looked like a branch lying on the trail. I guessed it wasn't a branch. And I guessed they were both terrified of snakes.

"How'd you get up there?" Mary Jane asked.

"We climbed," Angela said. "Now what do we do?"

I didn't really know. "Maybe snakes can't climb," I said hopefully. "Start going across."

They tried to scramble across the side of the cliff toward us. Rocks and dirt slid down under their feet. The snake didn't move.

As Angela grabbed hold of larger rocks and dug her shoes in, she managed to get closer to us and farther away from the snake. Mark climbed sideways and scrambled toward us too. Suddenly a large rock gave way under his feet and rolled down the cliff. It just about hit the snake head on. The snake slithered away with amazing speed. Mark started to slide down the cliff face on his rear end, hollering as he went. He was dangerously close to the edge of the drop-off Jeff had warned us about.

"Mark!" Mary Jane hollered. "Come this way, not to the right!"

Mark clung to the side of the hoodoo. "I can't move," he called. "Come get me!"

I looked at him in disbelief. "You're kidding, right? I'm not coming up there!

You come down here!" But I could see by the look on his face that Mark was not okay. So I carefully stepped off the trail. I slid down the ditch on the side of the trail and then clambered up the muddy side of the hoodoo. I reached Angela first. I clutched her shorts and urged her to let go and slide down. She finally did, and I held her hand and helped her down to the trail.

Then I looked back up at Mark. He hadn't budged. He looked pale. So I took a deep breath and started to clamber slowly up the side of the hoodoo. "What's wrong?" I asked when I got closer to him.

Mark swallowed. "I'm scared of heights," he whispered.

I followed his glance down to the drop-off on the other side and felt sorry for him. "Don't look down there," I told him firmly. "Here, I've got you." Which wasn't really true, but I grabbed his ankle and talked him into moving his hands down.

"Look at this rock—it feels like a handle," Mark said.

It didn't look like a rock to me. I took one more step higher to get a closer look. I scraped Mark's handhold with my nail. "Dude," I whispered, "that's not a rock— that's a bone!"

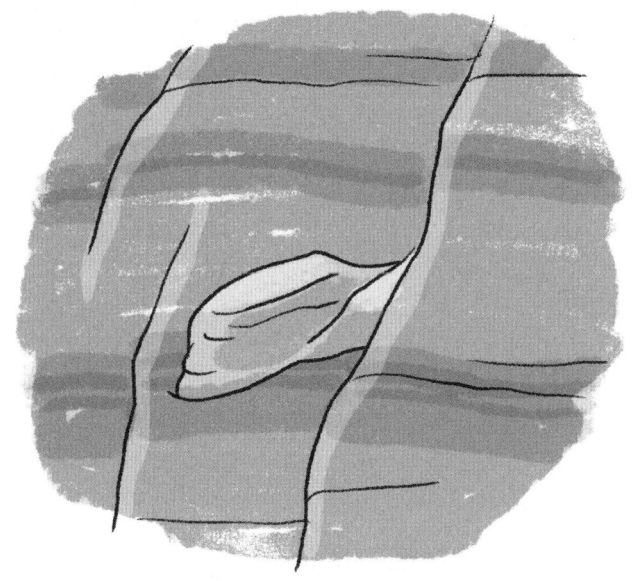

Mark wasn't too interested. He tried to find another hold. Slowly, step by step, I talked him down. Once we got closer to the trail, Mark could breathe again. We slid the last few meters on our bottoms. Mary Jane and Angela hauled us back onto the trail.

"Guys," I said, "I think Mark was holding on to a bone up there! A large bone!" The others looked at me blankly. "As in dinosaur-big bone!" I added. "I think we should tell Jeff about it."

"We can't tell him that we left the trail!" Mark said.

Angela looked at us all and started to laugh. "Don't you think they can tell that we didn't stay on the trail?" We looked at ourselves and realized we were covered in mud.

Just then Adam and Alex and Dudley came around the bend, and Mary Jane told them about my heroic rescues. But she didn't mention the bone. Adam and Alex looked impressed. Dudley just kept searching for the snake. He was crawling around calling, "Here ssssnakie, sssnake!"

I looked at Mark and shook my head. Neither one of us said a word about our discovery.

CHAPTER SEVEN

By the time we got back to the trailhead and the bus, Mrs. Cupcake and Mr. Jenkins were just about to start searching for us. Mrs. Cupcake took one look at us and screeched, "What have you been doing? Where have you been?"

Jeff frowned. We were caked in mud. Our shoes, pants and hands were an orangey brown.

Angela started to explain. "They saved us!" she said, pointing at Mary Jane and me. "We got attacked by a snake!"

Mrs. Cupcake let out a gasp. "Did you get bitten?" she asked.

"No," said Angela, "but it came really close. I was so scared. It chased us, so we had to get off the trail. Then we were stuck on this steep cliff, and Josh rescued us!"

Mrs. Cupcake looked at me much kindlier now. "Thank you for helping them, Josh," she said.

"I hope you didn't do any damage," Jeff mumbled.

"Do you want to check? Can I show you where it was?" I asked eagerly. I wanted to talk to Jeff about our discovery privately. Angela must have caught my drift because she started to go toward the bus, with most of the class in tow, telling the snake tale in great detail. Already it sounded like a boa constrictor.

"I have to show you something," I whispered to Jeff. He looked at me and realized I was serious. "Okay," he said. He called to the group, telling them to wait by the bus. "I want Josh to show me where this happened. We'll be back in just a few minutes."

We started back up the trail. "What's up?" Jeff asked as soon as we were out of earshot.

"I think we found something," I panted, trying to keep up to his long strides. "I climbed up the side of the hoodoo to where Mark was and there was this rock sticking out of the cliff. Only it wasn't a rock."

Jeff glanced at me sharply. "What was it?"

For an archeological kind of guy, he wasn't too bright. "Bone," I said. "I think it is dinosaur bone."

Jeff increased his speed and pretty soon saw where we had climbed. "Hmmm," he said, surveying the hoodoo we had scrambled up.

"There, see that bit that sticks out? It isn't rock. And there are no trees, so it's not a root."

"Hmm," Jeff said again. He left the trail, stepped down the ditch and then up the side of the hoodoo toward the cliff. "You stay there!" he ordered over his shoulder. I watched him clamber up alongside the muddy tracks we had left and scratch the same place I had. In no time he came back.

"You were right—that is no rock," he said once he was back on the trail, slapping me on the shoulder. "You may just have made a discovery there, boy!" Then he let out a roaring laugh. "All the time I've worked here I haven't found anything, and you, a kid from the city, find this! Must have been the rain." He shook his head and laughed again. "Nature has no favorites, I guess."

I felt excitement bubbling up inside my stomach. "I did? I really discovered dinosaur remains? You didn't know they were there?" I asked him in disbelief.

"No. Of course, we know that they can be anywhere here, but no, we never know where they might be discovered next, if at all."

I felt a tingle down my spine. I, Josh Jamieson, had discovered a dinosaur bone!

"What will happen now?" I asked as we started to head back toward the group.

"Well," Jeff said, "I'll come back with our chief paleontologist. We'll get him to confirm, and then we'll start excavating."

"Everything okay?" Mr. Jenkins asked when we got back to the bus.

"Yes, very well," Jeff said with a laugh in his voice, but that was all that he said. He looked at me and added, "You can't go on the bus like that!"

I guessed I did look pretty bad, all caked in mud. He made me strip down to my boxer shorts. He waved away my protests, saying, "If you were swimming, you'd look like that too." On the bus, everybody was killing themselves laughing.

Only the thought that I had made a great discovery let me live through this. "Just wait," I growled at Mark as I got on the bus in my underwear. "Just wait, and we'll see who gets the last laugh." I could tell he was dying to know what Jeff had said about the bone.

CHAPTER EIGHT

The following night Jeff came to our camp. We had just finished dinner in the cafeteria. We had corn on the cob and ham. The mashed potatoes were pretty gross, and we had flicked more off our forks than we had actually eaten. We were piling up the dishes when he walked in, accompanied by a man with gray hair.

All my friends were surprised to see Jeff again. I wasn't.

Jeff called us all together. "Hey, everybody," he said, "this is Dr. Johansen. He is our chief paleontologist." He singled me out. "Ken, this is Josh."

I could see Mrs. Cupcake wondering what I had done this time. I smiled and shook hands with Dr. Johansen. He looked at me and smiled too.

"Well, young man," he said in a deep voice, "you may have strayed from the path and you may have had to get on a bus in your underwear"—he winked at Jeff—"but you also made quite a discovery."

The whole class looked puzzled and crowded around us. Mr. Jenkins looked at me, obviously wondering what it was I had done to warrant this visit. "This young man," Dr. Johansen started to explain, "discovered a new dinosaur site."

There was a second of silence before everybody started talking at once.

"Josh did??"

"He did what?"

"How?"

"Where?"

"When?"

Dr. Johansen put up his hand to silence everyone and then told the story of what had happened. He told the part of the rescue pretty accurately, so he must have talked to Jeff about all that too.

"It wasn't just me," I interrupted. "If that snake hadn't been there, Mark and Ang wouldn't have left the trail, and then we'd never have seen the bone."

Dr. Johansen nodded and then told us how they'd gone back and identified the bone. He said that dating and excavating would begin soon.

"What kind of dinosaur was it?" Dudley wanted to know.

"Will they call it a Joshosaurus?" Mark yelled.

"I don't think we'll go that far," Dr. Johansen replied. "While it is never a good idea to go off the path when you have been told not to do so, we know

that circumstances, like rain and a snake, were beyond your control. So we would like to honor your discovery."

He smiled at me and then addressed Mr. Jenkins and Mrs. Cupcake. "We would like to name that specific site after your school. We'd like to name it the Pleasant Valley Excavation Site."

Mr. Jenkins looked pleased and proud. "Wait till we tell Principal Smart about this!" he said, grinning.

Mrs. Cupcake positively beamed. "Well," she exclaimed, "this has certainly been a memorable field trip!"

Dr. Johansen said there would be a sign at the site with the school's name on it. Then he proceeded to give us something even better. "I have here a gift certificate for your entire class," he said, "to the local pizza parlor. Tomorrow night you may all dine at Chunky Cheese Pizza at our expense!"

A roar went up from the group. Dudley slapped me on the shoulder, and Jesse hugged me. My friends put me on their shoulders and carried me around the dining room. Then they almost dropped me when Jeff called goodbye.

We watched as the paleontologists put up the sign at the site the next day, making our school as immortal as a dinosaur.

"This is great!" Mark said. "We saved our whole school from extinction!"

Dudley overheard him and grinned. "I told you our school had something to do with dinosaurs!" He was referring to a poem he had written about our teachers being as old as fossils.

Before we left Drumheller, we stopped at the pizza parlor to gorge on deep-dish pepperoni-and-salami pizza. The owner seemed pleased that we honored his place with a visit. Dr. Johansen must have paid him well—he kept refilling our glasses with soda and putting new steaming-hot pizzas on our tables. I pulled stringy cheese off with my teeth. Dudley collected everybody's olives. I ate pizza until I thought I'd explode.

That night we shone flashlights around our cabin and told ghost stories. Dudley was by far the best at making up stories. We tried to sneak outside and scare the girls, but Mr. Jenkins stopped us in our tracks and made us go back to bed.

Mrs. Cupcake came to tell us that she had phoned Mr. Smart and that the local newspaper wanted to interview us about our fossil discovery. We were going to be famous!

"Next thing we know they'll want to make a movie about us!" Mark laughed. "Yes, *Jurassic Pleasant Valley!*" Dudley chuckled.

The next morning we all climbed back onto the school bus for the trip home. Most of the kids were wearing new dinosaur caps and dinosaur T-shirts. I pulled some grape bubble gum out of my pocket. It would be a long drive, but going to the Badlands had definitely been a memorable experience. I climbed onto the bus and slid into the seat next to Mark. Funny, I thought, how dinosaurs can still have an impact today.

Margriet Ruurs is the author of many award-winning books for children. She enjoys speaking about reading and writing to students at schools around the world. Her adventures have taken her to such countries as Myanmar, Pakistan, Laos, Tanzania and many others. Margriet was born in the Netherlands but has been a Canadian for most of her life. She lives with her family on Salt Spring Island, British Columbia. For more information, visit margrietruurs.